TO

_____

FROM

_____

DATE

_____

DEAR SOLDIER
Heartfelt Letters from America's Kids

Originally published by Integrity Publishers, now owned by and published
in Nashville, Tennessee, by Thomas Nelson Publishers.

Thomas Nelson titles may be purchased in bulk for educational, business, fund-raising,
sales or promotional use. For information, please e-mail SpecialMarkets@ThomasNelson.com.

Cover and interior design: Greg Jackson,
Thinkpen Design, LLC, www.thinkpendesign.com

ISBN 1-59145-480-8
ISBN 978-1-59555-213-6 (CU)

14 15 16 17 18 RRD 11 10 9 8 7 6 5 4 3

Printed in the United States of America

DEAR ★ SOLDIER

I'm praying for you every day!

THOMAS NELSON
Since 1798

NASHVILLE DALLAS MEXICO CITY RIO DE JANEIRO

BARBARA WARFIELD BALDWIN

AMBER BALDWIN D'AMICO AND DR. HEATHER BALDWIN DUFF

Dedication

*This book is dedicated to the courageous men
and women of Operations Enduring and Iraqi Freedom
and to the families who have stood behind them.*

We thank you and salute you.

Acknowledgments

A portion of the proceeds from this book will be donated to the cause of wounded soldiers and veterans.

Thank you to the children who created these letters and pictures—and to their parents who gave permission for their work to be included in this book. This book would not have been possible without the support of teachers and staff from the following schools and organizations:

John H. Amesse Elementary School, Denver, Colorado; Galva-Holstein Elementary School, Holstein, Iowa; Lockport Elementary School, Lockport, Louisiana; J. I. Barron Elementary School, Pineville, Louisiana; Pontotoc Elementary School, North Pontotoc Elementary School, South Pontotoc Elementary School, and D.T. Cox Elementary School, all from Pontotoc, Mississippi; St. Matthew Catholic School, Franklin, Tennessee; Brookhaven Country Club Child Development Center, Dallas, Texas; Mound View Elementary School, Elk Mound, Wisconsin

We would also like to thank Mark Gilroy and Byron Williamson of Integrity Publishers; our agent, Leslie Nunn Reed, Nunn Communications, Inc.; Greg Jackson, Thinkpen Design, LLC; Steve and Jeannine Lee, Quicksilver Interactive Group, Inc.; Hopkins and Associates, Inc.; and countless others who have provided encouragement and support along the way.

Dear Soldier . . . Thank You!

Over the course of Operations Enduring Freedom and Iraqi Freedom, a group of faithful volunteers met weekly in Pontotoc County, Mississippi, to assemble care packages for our troops. The packages included personal care items and heartfelt letters of support from children.

Because the children's letters were so compelling, we would read them aloud as the packages were assembled. Their innocent wisdom and humor never failed to brighten and enrich our days. We soon started receiving feedback from soldiers telling us how much they appreciated the letters. Our own son and brother, who is an Apache helicopter pilot, said that letters like these meant the world to him while he was deployed.

An idea was born. Why not compile some of these letters into a book to be shared with active troops, veterans, military families, and the public? Coming from a family of soldiers, veterans, and Department of Veterans Affairs employees, we have seen up close and personal the depth of sacrifices made to protect our freedom. We wanted to create a book that would uplift our troops' spirits and express our gratitude.

We hope every reader finds as much comfort and inspiration in these letters as we have. Please join us in thanking our troops by sending your own letters to soldiers at our Web site, www.mydearsoldier.com.

God bless our troops and God bless America.

Barbara, Amber, & Heather

Dear soldier, September 2, 2004

I am glad that you are fighting for us. We are very happy. We hope you come back home safly. I hope we win. I sow a bunch of soldiers at the parade. I will pray for you. That will help you in Iraq.

Love, Blake

Ben

Pontotoc,
MS.
sept. 29, 200

Dear Soldiers,

How are you? I hope you are not geting hert. I hope you can read my hand writing because I'm doing the best I can. I hope you are ok right now. My name is Regina. I am 8 years old. I love school. It's my faverit thing. I like Apple Pie. My mom has got me to likeing it. I have brown eyes and brown hare. I like riding bikes. I have no pets because they want let us.

Your Friend,
Regina

DT. Cox school
MS PT 38863
September-7-04

Dear Soldiers,
   I hope that yall find that
Osama Bin ladin because he did
stuff that I could not imagin
so you might think I'm stupid but
I made it to forth grade so I make
A's and B's so there
                        Your friend,
                        Bowen

First Grade
                  Laken

Dear Soldier,

I am very startled by the amount of courage and bravery you have shown to your country. You are a shining star to all children and me too. You are sacraficing your own life for others. That to me is the most courageous thing in the world. Thank you!

Your friend,
Alex

God Bless
America
!

Golden
Eagle

February 9, 2005

Dear Soldiers,
Hello. My name is Christian. I like to build Legos and read Calvin & Hobbes.

Thank you so much for fighting for our freedom. My parents pray for you a lot. You may have known the man who died in the helicopter crash. He was from Cherokee, IA. We live in Galva, a short distance away. I've lived here about half my life. When I was 5, we moved from Flora, Illinois.

Try not to get hurt, OK? One thing the earth doesn't need is more hurt people.

Sincerely,
Christian

Blue springs, Ms 38828
September 28, 20

Dear American Soldier,

Hello. My name is Chandler Steele. I go to North Pontotoc Elementary. I am 9 years old and I'm in third grade. My favrite thing to do is break dance. My favrite singers are the Baja Men. I have a little brother and two nice parents.

Now that you now about me, I what to learn about you. What is your name? Are you scared? How long have you been in the Army? How do you take a bath?

I just want to say thanks for steping up.

Your friend,
Chandler

P.S. write me back.

Dear Soldiers,

My name is Scott. I have very bad hand writing. My father is a pilot for the National Guard. My father works at the hospital also. What do you eat over there?

Sincerely,
Scott

I pledge

allegiance

the flag...... to

Thanks, ★
For helping our contry.
I am 9 years old.
            your friend,
            Shannon
            TX

Dear soldier,

1-24-200[?]

My name is Creo. How is
it thar? It is snowey
hear. I'm 7 years old.
How old are you?
I dont figt. I like
to hant. Love, Creo

September 7, 2004

Dear soldier,

Hi my name is Gabriella.
I am nine years old in the
fourth grade. I go to D.T.
cox Elementary school.
I just wanted to thank
you for what all you have
done. I am proud that you
are defending our country
in Iraq because of your
bravery. I can ride my bike
and I can swimm swing, jump on my
Trampoline. Remember on your worst
day be good on your best day
be great.

Your Friend,
Gabriella

I go to school at J.I. Barron. I'm eight years old. I like riding my bikes. Hamburgers are my favorite food. My favorite hobby is basketball and football. I'm going to tobbe nine years old soon. I like videogames. There are many videogames I like to play. My dad's friends are in the army. There Soldiers. There in a big war. Thank you for protecting us.

Love, Nicholas,

Dear Soldier,
    Thank you for fighting for our country's freedom. You must have been very courageous to go and fight over there. Thank you for risking your life for us.

From,
Preston

February 9, 2005

Dear Soldier,

How are you doing over there? I'm fine. Thank you for going to Iraq and fighting for peace between Iraq and the United States. I hope you come home soon. I miss you lots. You are very brave people going and fighting for our country. I'm praying for you everyday. God is always with you. Deep down in my heart I know your doing as hard as you can to save our country. My name is Dana and I go to Galva-Holstein Elementry School. I really like to play football. Happy Valentine's Day!!

Your Friend,
Dana.

Piercer
D.T. Cox Elementary,
Ponbtoc, MS 38863

Dear Solider,

I don't know who will get this man
or woman whoever does God Bless You.
Thank you for going and putting your life
at risk for our country. (The United States)
I am keeping you in my prayes. I
hope you don't die. I don't know what
you are Navy, Army, Airforce, National Guard,
or Marines. Thank you for being what you
are. My best friend's name is Joshua Duff.
His Uncle Ben is in the airforce. I hope
he will be okay. I will keep him in my
prayers. I know the war is scary and
I know most all of you are scared. I hope
this letter from me will make you fill
at home. I hope this letter will make you
a little less scared. I love you whoever
you are and who ever gets this letter
please don't die. If you do die with
my letter so that will let the world know
that I care for each and every one
of you out there in the war. Thank you

Elizabeth Ann

Sep. 1, 2004

Dear Soldier,
    I know you are doing a great job in the war. You're perfecting your family and us. I hope you are safe and get good rest for the war. Any place you go you have each other. You men and weman are like family.

           Your Friend,
           Kate
           Pontotoc, MS
P.S. I'm in 3rd grade.

Dora

John Amesse

Colorado

level 5

April 28, 2005

To Soldiers

Dear Soldiers,

Hello my name is Dora Mazariegos. I am a student here at John Amesse Elementry School 5th grade in Mr. Walkers class. Have you ever gotten hurt badly? Can you tell me a little bit about your weapons. Do you see mosquito when you fight? What do you like to do? What do you like to eat? How is the weather? Do you have pets? Be safe

I hope you send me back really soon!

Sincerly,
Dora

September 7, 200

Dear Soldier,
My name is Kristen   and I
am nine years old. I go to D.T. Cox School
and I'm in the fourth grade. I just wante
to thank yall for fighting for our country
to give us freedom. I hope you will
have a nice day of training and fighti
I know yall have a great chance of
winning the war. Thank yall for letting
us have freedom thats what I'm trying
to say. Because of your bravery we
can live a happy life.

Sincerely,
Kristen

Kaylin F.
Age 7
Lockport, La

Dear Soldier,

My name is Kaylin.
I now how to shot a bebe gun.
Do you ride a dirtbike?
I am prownd of you.
I go to the school Lockport Lower.
Do you have yelloiwish grass grass.
My favrit fod is stack.
I live in lockport, La.
We hare flag raising.

Love Kaylin

Dear Soldiers,

I hope you win the war. Are whole class is praying for you. You are the best people for fighting for us. I hope it is a nice in Iraq. I hope you have comf beds. I want to be in the war just like you. I think you are brave to be in the war. Have you had any tornados? I am in first grade. my name is Brennan. I am a boy. My teacher is named Mrs. Bain. She is the best. You rock! My faviort sport is doge ball. I have a cat named mi (shes not that mini shes fat) I also have a kitten named Shadow. I like kittens. I am 7 years old. Is the weather hot or cold? I'm sorry that you miss your family. I miss my family too. Do you like being in the war? I bet you are very very nice I love you all. Do you have a lot of clothes? Have you met any freinds? I hope the war will end soon. Take care of your self. I am thankful for you. You are kind. Love, Brennan

Hi,

This is Ashley I was wondering what ya'll were doing. I am having a great time. Well, Ole Miss and Mississippi State are playing against each other. The Bodock Festival was last Friday and Saturday I had a great time. Dr. Kaylor, how are you? I am doing fine. I have been talking to your wife and Kids. Well, Pontotoc and South Pontotoc were against each other. Well guess who won? South-Pontotoc beat us. I am praying for you in my prayers.

Love Ashley

Dear, Soldier,
    We will pray for you. So don't worry and we mean
what we pray. We are proud what you are doing.
You are fighting for you people. So be proude. So
what say do what you came to do.

                    Love
                    Lakyn
                        3ra grand
                    Pontotoc, ms

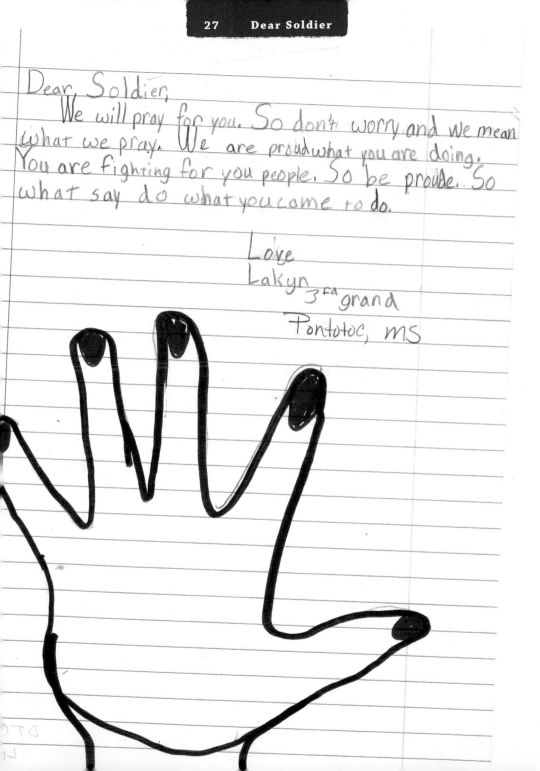

September 7, 2004

Dear, Soldier

Hellow my name is Wesley. I bet that Iriak is very deadle. But you wear brave enef to go up there and fite for our cortry! I could not fite up there because I can not stad blodey stuff.

Your friend.,
Wesley

Dear Soldier
    Where does a General keep his armies? UP his sleevies!\
    My name is Austin Dean Gregory. I am 8 years old and in the third grade. I live in Ecru, Mississippi with my mother and brother. I like to swim, ride my bike and ride horses. Thank you for defending our country
            God Bless America
                Austin

February 2, 2005

Dear Soldier,

Hi, my name is Maddison. I am ten years old, I go to Galva-Holstein. I appreciate you fighting for our country, so keep on fighting. I hope you get home to your family safely.

Sincerely,
Maddison
Holstein, Iowa

Pinevillie La. 71360
February 3, 2005

Dear Soldiers,

Thank you for going to war. My name is Amy. I like cabbage and pizza. I have two brothers, no sisters a cat, bird, and fish. I have a lot of friends. How can you live without T.V.? I hope you get home safely.

Sincerely,
Amy

Jhon

8 Yeasold

Lockport
Lower

Dearsoldier Are youe
in Irag. will lou get
to go home For December.
What do you do in Irag.
Do you Drive a armtanks.
I hope lou are safe.
Wath gine of gun do
lou have is it a
Machinegun. take you
for freeing the use
stamof Aimek. I fill
sad. will lou get to
come home for voletimesday.
I hope lou make it
home. If you free Amimk.
Faked lou for feeing us.
I hop lou get some
Oil. Your fried,
John

February 9, 2005

Dear Soldier,

Thank you for fighting for our country and saving our lives. I hope none of you have gotten hurt yet. I'm really glad for what you are doing for us. Hi! I'm Kaitlin from Galva Holstein Elementry School. I really like it here. I've been praying for you guys every night for you to be ok.

Sincerly,
Kaitlin

ECRU
September 28, 2004

Dear soldiers,

How are you doing? I hope you're winning your battles. Try not to get injured. We thank you for helping to keep our country safe and protecting our freedom. Please come home safely. When I grow up I wont to be a soldier.

Sometimes it is hot. Sometimes it is cold. Sometimes it is normal. I like it when it is normal. Do you?

Your Freind,
Josh

Dear soldiesrs,
I hope your haveing a grate time.
I'll pray fore you.
God bless you.

your friend, Claire

North Pontotoc Elem.
Pontotoc, Ms

october 6, 2004

Dear Soldier,

My name is Holly
I'm eight years old. I'm going
to ask you some questions.
Are you coming home for Thanksgiving?
Do you have a family?
Is this your first time
in the war? Now I'm going
to tell you about some stuff.
My new cousin's sister is in
the war her name is Robin.
your really missing the fall
leaves. Every body is picking
out halloween costums and
picking out pumkins. What
branch of the war are you
in? Your being so brave
to go out and fight for
our freedom! Do you ever
get nerves in the night
that some one is going to
sneak up on you?

Your truly
Holly

Pinevillie La. 7136(
February 3, 20(

Dear Soldiers,

Thank you for going to war.
My name is Amy. I like cabbage and
pizza. I have two brothers, no sisters
cat, bird, and fish. I have a lot of
friends. How can you live without
I hope you get home safely.

Sincerely,
Amy

February 3, 200

Dear Soldier,

I'm 10 years old. I'm in 4th grade at Galva-Holstein Elementary School. I'm thanking you for saving our country. I hope you come home soon. I hope your family is doing well. I hope you stay safe.

Sincerely
Josh

Dear Soldier

Ameris
Age 7
Lockport ILe

We hav flag raising in ore sch
My name is Ameris. you are fight
for ore world. For Friday we
say the pleg. And we now ole
the was to. Im proud to be in
American. I love being in America,
Be safe for evere. God bles

love Ameris American!

Dear Soldier, September 2, 2004

I am glad that you are fighting for us. We are very happy. We hope you come back home safly. I hope we win. I sow a bunch of soldiers at the parade. I will pray for you. That will help you in Iraq.

Love, Blake

Pineville LA 713
January 27, 200_

Dear Soliders,

Thank Thankyou for being ther to fight for us
I am nine and will be ten on Dec
6. I go to J.I Barron Elementry. I
think Iam pretty as a flower.
I am will really disappointed becau
my dad will not let my have a little do
I think my mom is on my side becaus
she says I can have a little dog in the
summer.
How was you week? You can
write back if you want. Oh, and
are all soliders boys?

Sincerly,
Taylor

February 2, 2005

Dear Soldiers,
I really appreciate you fighting for our liberty. Thank you for protecting our country. I hope you stay safe and come home soon. I am proud to have you fighting for us. Thanks again.

Sincerely,
Gretchen
age 10
Holstein, Iowa

P.S. I am proud to be an American

1-24-05 Jan. 24, 2005

Dear Soldier,

I have 3 pets. 2 of them our rabbits. I have 1 sister and 1 brother. 1 rabbit is my sisters. My sister name is Amanda. she is 9 My brother name is colton. hes 2. My name is David. Im 8. Im in 2nd grade. My 3 pet is a hammster. it's name is Peanut. the rabbit that is mine is Mie. My sisters rabbit's name is Elizabeth.

love, David

P.S. I hope you come back safely.

September 7, 2004

Dear Soldier,

I hope you get to come home soon. I am in the third grade. My mamas name is Cathy my daddys name is Bill I have a brother to his name is Kyle. My faviort animal is a dog. I have a dog we bought him a shirt it sayes Ruff stuff. I have two cats. But I uses to have five but we had to give them away. My dogs name is Dusty. My cats name is Blacy and Socks. I Love animals. My grand-mother has canser her name is Jane.

Love, Kayla

Dear Soldiers,
    Thank you for fighting for
our freedom. I know it is hard
because My mama's daddy was in
the war, and his name is
William   He was in the
war when he was eighteen.
He survived. My brother says that
he wants to be in the war. I'm
thinking I might join him. Thank
you all for fighting for us.

    from: William

I pledge alegance to the flag
of the united states of America
into the rebublic for witches
stands one nation under God
indivisible in Liberty and justice
for all

ERICA

Pineville, La 71360
February 3, 2005

Dear Soldiers,

Do you have any friends? I have a lot of friends here. My friends are there for me. They are really nice people. Some are tall like a house, and some are short. But I like them anyway.
I am happy you are fighting for your country. Good luck!

Sincerely,
Emily

NPE School
8324 Hwy 15 N.
Ecru, Ms 38841
Oct. 4, 2004

Dear Soldier,
My name is Tristan. I'm eight years old. I'm in the 3rd grade. Do not be afraid God is watching over you and I'm praying for you, too. Thank you for supporting our country.

Your friend,
Tristan

February 9, 2005

Dear Soldiers,
    I hope we win the war. My cousin is in the army. I wish he could come back and all of you guys too. I'm wondering if its hot or cold there. I'm ten years old and I'm from Iowa. I like to farm. Thank you for saving our country.

Love,
Dustin

Dear Soldier,   1-24-05

If you get hurt make sure you get to a Docter. My name is Tim. I Live in Elk Mound, Wisconsin. I Live in the country.

Love,
Tim

I thic you all are herros. ♥ILA

TEXAS

4/29/05

Dear Soldiers,

Thank you for going to Iraq to fight for us. I go to St. Mattew School. My dad was in the navy. I will pray for you.

Love Mary

P.S. I am praying

Dear Soldiers,

Thank you for fighting for our country. When ya'll come back we will give ya'll more spirit, becauce we love ya'll. I hope you live because some of my classmates' parents are with you. So my classmates and I just wanted to say good luck, and we miss you and love you in our heart. God does too. I am counting on ya'll and I can't wait for you to back. My teache teaches us everything we know and my classmate and I love her. We love all of the teacher. right back.

Love,
Shaketa

Mrs. eithre Age8 chockport La

I like to be a soldier but my mom dot let me.

I have a b-b gun I like it oneday I will be a soldier.

I hurd a helicedcer crase I shik 8 soldien. I am sade I hope you dint have a frande my name is Joshua.

Holstein, IA 51025
Feb. 11, 2005

Dear American soldiers,
     I am nine in third grade going to be
ten June 19th. I live North west Iowa. I like
basketball, video games, and math. I have a
dog named Elvis. I live on a big farm with
lots of pigs. Thank you for saving our
country and our lives.

                    Sincerely,
                    Tyler
            Age 9 / 3rd grade
            Holstein, IA

Dear Soldiers

I am parying for you.
I hope you have a good time in Iraq.
Do you play the giutar?
Do you play footdall?
And I am in 1st grade.

from B.J.

P.S. Why was Cinderella sych a lousy soccer player? She had a pumpkin for a coach.

Dear Solders,   September 2, 2004

    I'm sorry you had to go to war. We are wearing ribbons today to sopport yall. We all are happy that you went to save our contry. But we are ready for yall to come home. I hope that yall are wining right now. We had a prade for yall to sopport yall. We hope that yall are safe right now. Yall are so nice to want to save our contry. We love yall. We are praying for yall every night and every morning.

Love,
Whitney

Nicolle

7

Lockport Lower

Dear Soldier,

Do you fight with guns? Are we wining? How are you? We are find. Thanks for making our contry a free one. Do you use swords to fight? Do you throw boms in Iraq. I hope you don't get hurt. Are you comming home for Mardi Gras. Is it causing a lot of damage? Do you fight with guns too? Are you doing good in the army?

Dear soldier,
        Thank-you for fighting in Iraq to make the world a better place. To me you are a real hero in my life. You make me confident in everything I do. You make me feel safe in what I do. I hope you will be all right out there and make it home to your familys. It is a brave thing that you are doing. Good luck.

                    With Love,
                    Ashley

Jordan
8
Lockporshon.

Dear Solider
I hope you are okay
I like Soliders I got little
men I a proud of you
I know you miss your famialy
I wish I can be in the
army but my mom says
it's to dangures so I
cant go in the army my
faviort tv shoh is fishing
my favorit sport is
fishing. you are the
braves men in the hole
wibe World.

I Hope you come Home safle and see yoerfamae soon

Brock Tx

519 E. Maple St.
Holstein, IA 51025
Feb. 11, 2005

Dear Soldiers,
    I am in third grade and I hope you guys win the war for us. I think it must be hard for all of you because you miss your families. I just can't believe there are 150,000 Americans fighting for our freedom. I just want to say thank you for all that you're doing and risking your lives for us.

Sincerly,
Keziah
9½   3rd grade
Holstein IA

Let us have Freedom!

Dear Soldiers,

Hi my name is Christopher Warfield. If you've met the maker of the book Barabara Warfield. She is m aunt. If you see the note by Preston Warfield. He's m brother. My grandfather was in the war his name Bob Warfield. Bi Solders.

P.S. Believe in your self.
P.S.S. I love monkeys.

Holstein, IA 51025
Feb. 11, 2005

Dear soldiers,
I'm in third grade in Holstein. My
favorite move is WHERE THE
RED FERN GROW. I like to go
ice fishing in the winter if I go
in the summer I'll fall in the
water. I saw a book a man
caught a big fish.

Sincerely, Jay   Age 8
third grade Holstein, Iowa

september 7, 200

American Solder,
I am Rubi
   I am glad I am an Mexican.
   We know that solders from pontotocare
   I Wish that the war ended quickly.
   I wonder if the war ends quickly.
   And specily I am in 3rd grade.
   I want you to know that my school
is DT. COX it is a pritty name. Anyway.
I hope you will besare. ~~I am~~ ~~now~~ ~~wi~~
~~are~~ ~~the~~
                              Yourtrend

thank   you for trying
to save   amarika.
Love,
   colton

Dear soldiers
I am Duncan. I
like to tell you something
thern is a paridise. You
can blelve me. You are cool

Dunca
n
Age 6
Look
port La

4-29-05

Dear Soldiers,
   I am glad you are fighting for
our country. I will be praying for
you. I hope the United States will win.
   I hope your are safe in Iraq. you
must be tuff.
                    from, Anne

Dear Soldiers,
Thank you for serving our Country.
My uncle is going to help with
the airplane to take off.
                    Love, Jesse

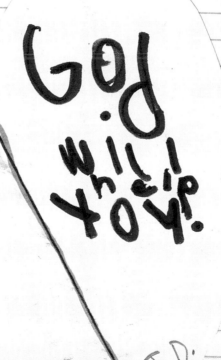

519 E. Maple
Holstein IA 51025
February 14, 2005

Dear Soldier,
    Thank you for serving us in the
Army. Your doing a lot of help. And I
think your family misses you. I hope you
don't get hurt. By the way my name
is Josey   My nickname is Jobug
because I like bugs. Your a brave person
in this country. Happy Valentinse day!

            Sincerely,
            Josey
            8 years old

Lexus
Age 8
Lockport LA

Dear Soldier

I hope you get to come
see your family. Thank you
for fightting for our war.
I will always pray for you
and your friends. I love you
throgh my hart always. Now
I can play outside without
watching for boms. My favrite
sport is baseball. My favrite
meal is hamburgers, frichfrise,
and meatpies. I hope you don't
get hurt. Remamber I will
always love you very very very
much. I will alway pray for
you and your friend.

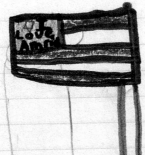

Love,
Lexus

4-29-0
WI

Dear Soldiers,
I'm very happy that you are fighting for
our country. I know Iraq is the bad side and
your the good side. I hope you win. I am praying a-
lot every day.

Your friend,
connor
P.S. What do you get when you cross
a skunk and a helacopter?
(Answer on side)

Dear Soldier,

Thanks for fighting for us. I hope you enjoy this letter. I pray that you have a safe return to your family. It is people like you who make America proud. You represent what America stands for. God bless you.

Sincerely,
Zach

519 E. Map
Holstein IA 510
February 14, 200

Dear Soldier,
    Thank you for serving us in the Army. Your doing a lot of help. And I think your family misses you. I hope you don't get hurt. By the way my name is Josey   My nickname is Jobug because I like bugs. Your a brave person in this country. Happy Valentines day!

       Sincerely,
       Josey
       8 years old

Dear Solider,
    I'm glade yall are over there to peartect us and I hope that all of yall come back safe. My brother is coming there soon and his name is James, And I want you to try to find him and give him my letter,

       Your friend,
       River

Dear Soldiers,

Do you know where Louisiana is? I do because I live there.

My name is Preston and I go to J. I. Barron.

Do you go to church? I do, because I am christon.

Were you baptized?

What is it liice on the desert?

Sencerely,
Preston

4-29-09

WI

Dear Soldiers,

Thank you for helping the U.S.A.
You must be brave.
When I was 5. I fell in my
boll of spetdy. Did you meet nev
friends? What has 18 legs, spits,
and catches flies? A baseball team.
P.S. Im 8   Love, Macy

Dear Soldier,

Thanks for fighting for us. I hope you enjoy this letter. I pray that you have a safe return to your family. It is people like you who make America proud. You represent what America stands for. God bless you.

Sincerely,
Zach

Dear Soldier,
I am a fourth grader at D. T. Cox Elementary in Pontotoc, MS. My name is Claylee   and I am 9 years old. I have a little brother named J.D. I have a cousin in Iraq, his name is Brad.

   Thank you for going to Iraq for our country. Because of your bravery I am able to live in a free country. A free country where red, white, and blue are our colors and God watches over us.

                              Sincerely,
                              Claylee

Jan. 24, 2005
1-24-05

Dear Soldier,

My name is Ariel.
I have 10 animals
3 dogs, 3 cats, 2 fishes, 1 bird
and a rabbit. I'm 8 years
old. I'm in second grade. I
hope you come home soon.
Love, Ariel

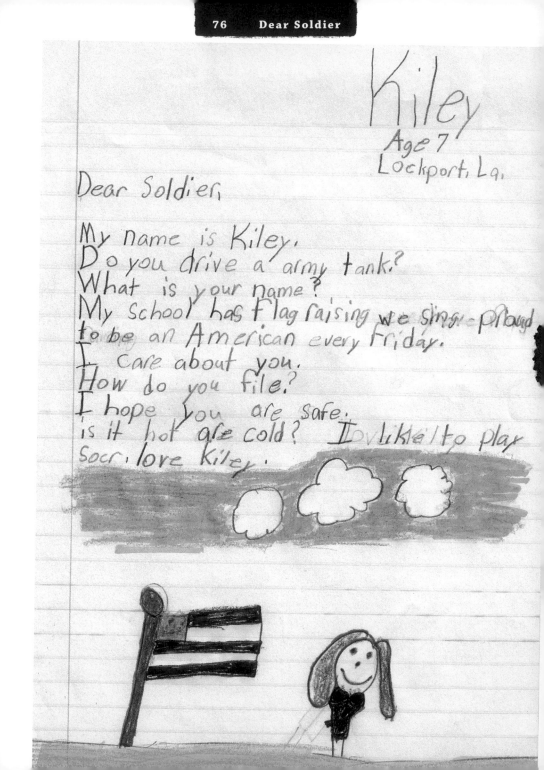

Kiley
Age 7
Lockport, La.

Dear Soldier,

My name is Kiley.
Do you drive a army tank?
What is your name?
My school has flag raising we sing proud
to be an American every Friday.
I care about you.
How do you file?
I hope you are safe.
is it hot are cold?   I ovliktilto play
Socr. love Kiley.

February 9, 2005

Dear Soldiers,

How have you guys been lately? Thank you for going to Iraq for us. I hope you guys aren't getting injured. I've been thinking and praying for you guys. God is always going to be with you. You guys are very brave people for fighting for the country. Hope you come home safely.

Sincerly,
Trista

November 18, 200⁶

Dear Soldier,

Every one in my family appreciates you! You are in our prayers, our dreams, and everywhere. You might be sad or lonely, but maybe this will cheer you up!

" I know that you are really sad
but this will make you really glad
We love you very very much
I bet that you can win in just a touch
You are doing a great thing
And when you win we will sing"

Kellon

Dear Solder,

Thank you for ricking your life to save us. I thank you from the boudom of my heart. And triy to hove a good time. g I give you all my prayers.

From,
Erica

God bless the American soldiers, Oh, let God be with you.

God Bless the USA!

Dear soldiers,

4-28-05

God bless
America

My name is Kristin   I'm
Years old and go to John Amesse Elem.
I'm just writing to thank you for
serving are country. How is it out there? Do
you have a lot of free time? I don't have
very much free time. I heard you guys/women
like movies. What's your favorite? Mine is
the cat in the Hat 3 Blade trinity. Do you
like cookies? My favorite is suger cookies
and choclate chip. Do you like being in the
army? I like the camoflage color. Do you have
any kids? I have 3 brothers 3 3 sisters. If so
whats their name? Well I am so thankful
that your out there. Your so brave. I want
to learn more about you. Write back

Sincerely,
Kristin      Colorado

Dear Soilder of Iraq,

I am writing to you to see how you are doing there.

My prayers are with you all for a safe return back to the states.

And I hope you can reach your families and Loved ones and I hope you can read my letter whoever you are and I am glad that you are protecting us and your families and Loved ones and your country.

And I hope that all of you over in Iraq can be safe and help people in Iraq to be safe and to save their country as well.

And I hope you have lots of cookies and DVD's to watch and I hope you get a Lot of Letters and mail to read.

from
Isaiah

9/7/04

Dear Soldier,
    I hope you come back soon. I am in the thrird grade. I think your are very brave to go fight. Maybe we could go ahead and just catch the bad guy's if we could. Even if I don't know you I still think you are the coolest.

Love,
Joshua

Kevin

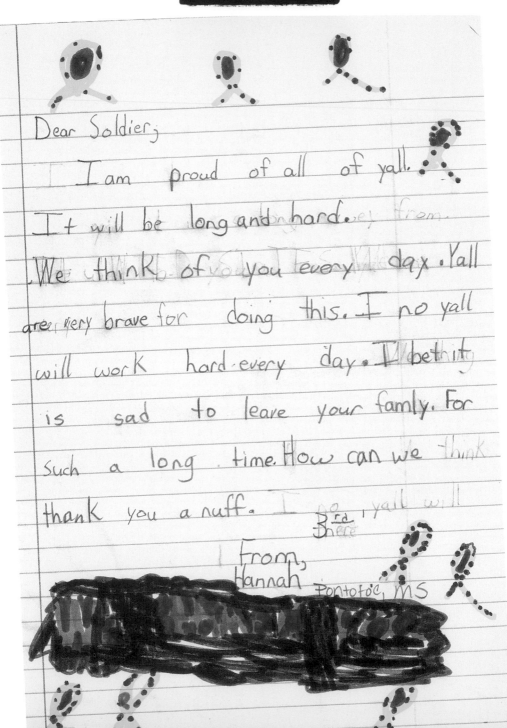

Dear Soldier,

I am proud of all of yall.

It will be long and hard.

We think of you every day. Yall

are very brave for doing this. I no yall

will work hard every day. I bet it

is sad to leave your famly. For

such a long time. How can we think

thank you a nuff. I no yall will

3rd here

From,
Hannah
Pontotoc, MS

Dear Soldier,

We know your going to do a great job! I know you miss your family members. I wrote to cheer you up. you are going to be a great Soldier. I will be thinking of you and praying for you.

From,
Merideth Kate

Pontotoc, MS

Let's Pray

Dear protector of the peace,   #15
    Thank you for fighting for our county. You probably wake up every day thinking will I live to see tommorrow. You and your fellow soldiers are probably the bravest people I know. When you're in battle do you get really nervous? I know I would never be brave enough to do what you're doing right now. Again thank you for everything you do!

                    God bless you,
                    James

Dear Soldier,   Pineville La.

My name is Richard. I am eight,
I go to school at JI. Barron.
My favorite food is Speghetie.
I live in Pineville La.
I am sorry your away from home.
I hope you win the war. Thank you for
all you do. I hope you get home soon.

                    Sinceraly
                    Richard,   Sept. 7, 2004

I am a fourth grader at P.T. Cox
Elementry in Pontotoc, MS. My name is
Trey and I am 9 years old. I
like to ride my four-wheeler and spend
time with my brother. Thank you for
going to Iraq for our country. Because of
your bravery I am able to play outside without
having to watch out fo bombs. And now
I can go to a place a lot safer.

                    Your friend,
                    Trey.

Febuary 9, 2005

Dear Soldiers,

Thank you for saving our lives. I'm Austin from Galva-Holstein, Elementary School in Iowa. I love to play with my figurines. What is it like up there? It's snowy down her. My cousin just got married and she and her husberd went to Iraq. Heres a detail of my self. Three days after Christmas my brother and I were playing around and I leaned on a loading shoot and it fell on my head. Two days after that I turned greenish yellowish and now I'm ok. Be safe and live.

Sincerly,
Austin

Dear American Solider, Ecru MS october 1, 2004

Hello. My name is Theresa ~~_____~~ I go to North pontotoc Elementry school. I am 8 years old. and I'm in the third grade. My favorite thing to do is Math.

Now that you know all about me, now I want to know about you. How long have you been in the milatary, How old are you? Who is your captain? Who is second in command? Do you have any friends? Are you scared?

I just want to say thank you for all that you do for our country. If it weren't for you our country would not be free. I'm glad that you step up and fight. You are my friend.

D.T. cox school,
Pontotoc MS, 38863
September 7, 2004

Dear soilders,
  I hope you guys can make it
throw the ocean and fight war
VS war. I also hope that you guys win
because I don't want you to die.

Nancy

Your friend
Keaton.

Camille
Age 6
Lockport, LA.

Dear Soldier, I care about you I wish you didn't die. In the raising we sing the song I'm proud to be a Amerrician. My name is Camille. Do you rid an army tank? What is your name? Is it hot or cold where you fite the war? What dose your heart feell like inside? Are you scared to fite the war? Thank you for fiting the war. The End.

I am saying the plage of aligeins.

Dear Solder,
   Thankyou for all the army does
for this country like stops freaky
teristoes from bombing the USA with
massive nuclear weapons, Like stoping
the terriost all across Irque, Thankyou
for all you dou

                    Tennessee,
                    Tyler
                    Thanks again

Thank You Soldiers !

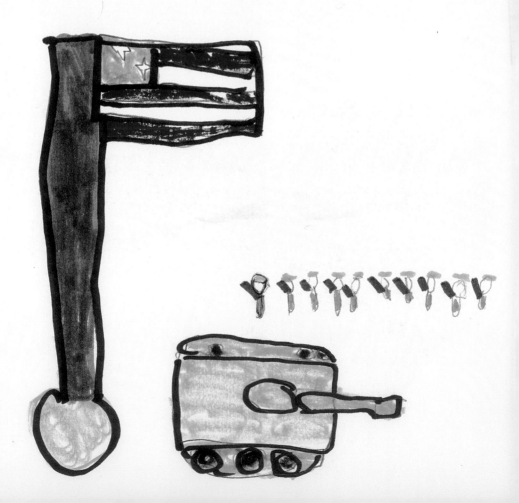

Dear soldier,
   I know you are serving in Iraq. You might know my cousin. She has black hair and is real tall. I live in Thaxton, Mississippi, and I'm proud to be an American.

Your freind
Sheldon

Thankyou for telling us be free, and this is for all you soldiers out there, god bless America!

Grade: 3rd
Name: Chelsie